# Passengers Onc
## New and reopened stations
## and lines since 1948

## SOUTHERN ENGLAND
### from Kent to Cornwall

Diesel unit No 158885 has just arrived at Southampton Airport Parkway from Salisbury on 23 May 2009. It has come via Romsey and Southampton Central and is heading for Romsey again, where it terminates (see page 52). The entrance to the airport is from the right-hand (down) platform.

# Passengers Once More

## New and reopened stations
## and lines since 1948

## SOUTHERN ENGLAND
## from Kent to Cornwall

### Terry Gough ARPS

Silver Link Publishing Ltd

© Terry Gough 2011

ISBN 978 1 85895 355 9

Silver Link Publishing Ltd
The Trundle
Ringstead Road
Great Addington
Kettering
Northants NN14 4BW

Tel/Fax: 01536 330588
email: sales@nostalgiacollection.com
Website: www.nostalgiacollection.com

Printed and bound in the Czech Republic

First published in 2011

British Library Cataloguing in Publication Data

A catalogue record for this book is available from the British Library.

# Abbreviations

| | | | | |
|---|---|---|---|---|
| **BluR** | Bluebell Railway | **LBSCR** | London, Brighton & South Coast Railway |
| **BR** | British Railways | **LCR** | Liskeard & Caradon Railway |
| **BR(W)** | Western Region | **LNER** | London & North Eastern Railway |
| **BR(S)** | Southern Region | **LNWR** | London & North Western Railway |
| **BWR** | Bodmin & Wenford Railway | **LSWR** | London & South Western Railway |
| **CTRL** | Channel Tunnel Rail Link | **MHR** | Mid Hants Railway |
| **DCR** | Devon & Cornwall Railway | **NSE** | Network South East |
| **DCRP** | Devon and Cornwall Rail Partnership | **P&P** | 'British Railways Past and Present' |
| **DMU** | Diesel multiple unit | **P&PC** | 'Past and Present Companion' |
| **DR** | Dartmoor Railway | **PDSR** | Paignton & Dartmouth Steam Railway |
| **DSR** | Dartmouth Steam Railway | **PMV** | Parcels & Miscellaneous Van |
| **DVR** | Dart Valley Railway | **SCRP** | Sussex Community Rail Partnership |
| **EKR** | East Kent Railway | **SDJR** | Somerset & Dorset Joint Railway |
| **EMU** | Electric multiple unit | **SDR** | South Devon Railway |
| **ESR** | East Somerset Railway | **SECR** | South Eastern & Chatham Railway |
| **FGW** | First Great Western | **SR** | Southern Railway |
| **GWR** | Great Western Railway | **SRCP** | Swale Rail Community Partnership |
| **HGV** | Heavy Goods Vehicle | **SVR** | Spa Valley Railway |
| **HS1** | High Speed 1 | **SwanR** | Swanage Railway |
| **IWCR** | Isle of Wight Central Railway | **SWT** | South West Trains |
| **IWCRP** | Isle of Wight Community Rail Partnership | **TDL** | Tarka & Dartmoor Lines |
| **IWR** | Isle of Wight Railway | **TSR** | Torbay Steam Railway |
| **IWSR** | Isle of Wight Steam Railway | **TTV** | Tamar & Tavy Valleys |
| **KESR** | Kent & East Sussex Railway | **WSR** | West Somerset Railway |

# Contents

# Bibliography

Baker, S. K. *Rail Atlas of Great Britain & Ireland*, 11th ed (OPC, 2007; ISBN 978 0 86093 602 3)

Bevan, A. *A-Z of Rail Reopenings* (Railway Development Society, 1998; ISBN 0 901283 13 4)

Butt, R.V. J. *The Directory of Railway Stations* (Patrick Stephens Ltd, 1995; ISBN 1 85260 508 1)

Clinker, C. R. *Great Western Railway – A Register of Halts and Platforms 1903-1979* (Avon-Anglia Productions, 1979; ISBN 0 905466 29 2)

Gough, T. A. *British Railways Past & Present No 18: Surrey & West Sussex* (Past & Present Publishing, 1993; ISBN 1 85895 002 3)

    *No 21: Berkshire & Hampshire* (Past & Present Publishing, 1994; ISBN 1 85895 042 2)

    *No 46: Kent* (Past & Present Publishing, 2004; ISBN 1 85895 238 7)

    *No 51: Isle of Wight* (Past & Present Publishing, 2005; ISBN 1 85895 179 8)

Gough, T. A. *Past & Present Companion: The Bluebell Railway* (Past & Present Publishing, 1998; ISBN 1 85895 129 1)

    *The Kent & East Sussex Railway* (Past & Present Publishing, 1998; ISBN 1 85895 149 6)

    *The Tamar & Tavy Valleys* (Past & Present Publishing, 2001; ISBN 1 85895 171 2)

    *The Tarka & Dartmoor Lines* (Past & Present Publishing, 1998; ISBN 1 85895 139 9)

    *The Tarka Trail* (Past & Present Publishing, 1998; ISBN 1 85895 140 2)

Gough, T. A. and Mitchell D. *British Railways Past & Present No 29: Dorset Part 1* (Past & Present Publishing, 1996; ISBN 1 85895 089 9)

    *No 44: Dorset: a Second Selection* (Past & Present Publishing, 2004; ISBN 1 85895 219 0)

Gray, P. W. *Past & Present Companion: The Paignton & Dartmouth Steam Railway* (Past & Present Publishing, 1994; ISBN 1 85895 047 1)

Mitchell, D. *British Railways Past & Present No 8: Devon* (Past & Present Publishing, 1991; ISBN 1 85895 058 9)

    *No 17: Cornwall* (Past & Present Publishing, 1993; ISBN 1 85895 060 0)

    *No 30: Somerset* (Past & Present Publishing, 1996; ISBN 1 85895 088 0)

    *No 52: East Devon* (Past & Present Publishing, 2005; ISBN 1 85895 211 5)

    *No 53: North & West Devon* (Past & Present Publishing, 2006; ISBN 1 85895 245 X)

    *No 54: East Cornwall* (Past & Present Publishing, 2006; ISBN 1 85895 244 1)

Morrison, B. and Beer, B. *British Railways Past & Present No 20: Kent & East Sussex* (Past & Present Publishing, 1994; ISBN 1 85895 044 9)

Morrison, B. and Brunt, K. *British Railways Past & Present No 7: North East, East & South East London* (Past & Present Publishing, 1991; ISBN 0 947971 55 6)

Quick, M. *Railway Passenger Stations in Great Britain* (Railway & Canal Historical Society, 2009; ISBN 978 0 901461 57 5)

Staines, D. *Spa Valley Railway* (Halsgrove Press, 2009; ISBN 978 1 84114 928 8)

Stretton, M. J. *Past & Present Companion: The Bodmin & Wenford Railway* (Past & Present Publishing, 1999; ISBN 1 85895 135 6)

    *The West Somerset Railway* (Past & Present Publishing, 2000; ISBN 1 85895 166 9)

Williams, D. J. *Past & Present Companion: The West Somerset Railway Vol 2* (Past & Present Publishing, 2009; ISBN 1 85895 258 1)

# Acknowledgements

The various heritage lines are thanked for providing lineside passes. I thank the staff of the Train Operating Companies for their help and advice on local matters. In particular I thank Julian Crow (First Great Western General Manager for the West of England). I am grateful to Hugh Davies ('Photos from the Fifties') for the photograph of Hardley Halt, Martin Lawrence for Ketche's Halt and the new East Grinstead Bluebell Railway platform, and to David Mitchell for Boscarne Interchange. All other photographs are by the author. I am grateful to John Hillmer, Roger Marsh and Colin Pattle, all of whom have made valuable comments in relation to the book. I also thank my wife Cynthia, who did not believe that some of the closed stations we had visited in our early years together would ever reopen. We had travelled by train from Esher to Templecombe on 28 June 1958, in order to begin a long cycle ride to Lands End. Once Templecombe closed, she thought that such an experience could never be repeated. The station has reopened, but she has declined my invitation to relive the cycle ride.

# Introduction

This is the first volume of a series of books that will in time extend across the whole of Great Britain. The area covered by each book is based on present-day county boundaries, and this volume includes Kent, Sussex, Surrey, Berkshire, Hampshire, Dorset, Somerset, Devon and Cornwall.

A commonly held view is that all reopened stations are characterless, with nothing more than a simple platform on which stands a structure resembling a bus shelter. While this is true for some stations, there are many that have good facilities and attractive buildings. In some instances, the buildings of the original railway company have been restored. In other cases, functional buildings of modern design have been built. There is much variety, as the reader will see in the following pages. What is striking is the amount of care and effort that has been put into restoring the stations on heritage lines. Virtually every station is attractive and well kept, reflecting the enormous amount of hard work that has been expended to achieve this. Some stations managed by the Train Operating Companies are also maintained to a high standard, with little additions such as hanging baskets, which add to their welcoming appearance. There are others that are rather bedraggled, either through lack of care or by vandalism. I am pleased to write that, whatever the condition of the station, I was courteously received everywhere I visited in the course of collecting material for this book.

As the title indicates, this book is about reopened stations and passenger lines. The period extends from 1948 to the present day, whether or not the facility is still open. In the course of research for the book, it became apparent that there were other interesting facets to new passenger services. The book therefore embraces other categories of stations and lines. Some lines, used only for freight or empty stock trains, have been redesignated to include passenger trains. This applies particularly to spurs and curves. These are included, whether or not there are any stations, an example being the West Byfleet Curve. There have also been a number of openings at locations where previously there never was a station, such as Lelant Saltings.

It is very unusual for new lines to be built, where previously there was no railway. The supreme example of this is the Channel Tunnel Rail Link (High Speed 1), part of which is covered in this volume. Another aspect of reopenings has been the conversion of traditional heavy rail lines to tramways, although there are none within the area covered by this first volume.

Dormant stations – those not formally closed but which no longer have a regular passenger service – are included. They may have occasional special passenger trains, an example in this volume being Folkestone Harbour.

There are instances of stations or lines being closed for engineering works or other reasons, then reopened. These have been included only when such closures have been for at least six months. This therefore excludes, for example, Yeovil Junction to Honiton, which was closed for only about a week at the end of 2009 to complete reinstatement of double track in the Axminster area.

Heritage railways are included only when a service is provided between at least two stations. Thus the Bluebell Railway is included, but the Lavender Line is not. Heritage railway centres are regarded as museums and are therefore not included.

Stations are sometimes built for a specific short-term need. Such temporary stations will be included in the series whenever possible, although information can be difficult to source. There are none in this category in this volume.

There are frequent reports of proposals to reopen more stations, but few have sound business cases or would give significant social benefits. One line that does have much support is that from Uckfield to Lewes, although there continue to be arguments about its viability. There are also periodic calls to reinstate the railway between Guildford (Peasmarsh Junction) and Cranleigh. Campaigns to reopen these two lines have been running for decades. It may be many years before such commendable schemes come to fruition and I have not therefore included them.

Serious consideration is being given to reinstating the old South Western main line over Dartmoor, from Beer Alston to at least

Tavistock, and it now seems very likely that this will come to fruition. Tavistock has therefore been included in this book. It is much more doubtful whether the line will ever be extended to Okehampton, desirable though this may be. This closure was seen by some at the time to be a bad decision and now, with the resurgence of rail travel (and problems in the Dawlish area with high seas) it is seen to be a significant mistake. The same applies to singling much of the South Western main line between Salisbury and Exeter. The cost of reopening stations such as Templecombe and adding passing loops far outweighs the short-term savings made in the 1960s and 1970s. A modest scheme that is likely to proceed is the building of a new 'parkway' station for the Looe branch, and this I have included.

Excluded from the series are conversions of standard-gauge lines to narrow-gauge, such as the Seaton Tramway. Also excluded are stations rebuilt to replace an older station on the same or a nearby site, where there was no break in the provision of passenger services – Polegate and Exmouth are examples. The only exception is where the new station has significantly enhanced facilities, as occurred with Eltham (see Passengers Once More Essex to Gloucestershire & London). Also excluded are those stations such as Kingswear, which transferred from state to private ownership (in BR days) without a break in service.

The dates of openings have been obtained from a variety of sources and there is occasional disagreement. In the case of heritage lines, there are several instances when stations were open to the public months or even years before passenger services began. I have taken the latter date. For all stations, I quote the date services began, not the date associated with any official ceremony, which may have taken place weeks or months later. Variations can also occur when the station did not have a Sunday service, so the last train ran on a Saturday. In one famous incidence the last train ran weeks before legal closure because of a rail strike. Variations also occur as some sources quote the last day of regular services and others the last day of all services. In the case of new or reopened lines, I quote the dates relevant to passenger services.

Many of the stations have 'friends' or similar support groups that contribute to maintaining a tidy environment and publicise the service. Some stations are covered by Rail Partnerships whose membership may include interested parties from the community, local government and other bodies. These organisations have been very useful and have given several lines a higher profile than hitherto.

## Using this book

The stations are listed in line order, from Kent to Cornwall. For each station the name is accompanied by the map reference in Baker's *Rail Atlas of Great Britain & Ireland* (see the Bibliography) – the page number followed by the grid reference. Some stations are not marked in the atlas, in which case the reference is shown in brackets. Then follow the various opening and closing dates, and references, where appropriate, to any other photographs of the station that have been published in Past & Present Publishing's 'British Railways Past & Present' and 'Past & Present Companion' series (again, see the Bibliography). Under 'Operator' are listed the owning company at the Grouping in 1923, and the current organisation managing the station (Train Operating Company or Network Rail), or the operator in the case of a heritage line. Where a station is no longer open, I have entered the name of the operator at closure. For reopened lines, the dates refer to use by passenger trains.

Terry Gough
Sherborne

PLEASE NOTE that details of train services given in this book are correct at the time of writing, but will vary in the future. Always check with the operator before travelling.

## Shepherdswell 14, A1

| | | |
|---|---|---|
| Previous name | Shepherd's Well | |
| Opened | 16 October 1916 | |
| Closed | 1 November 1948 | |
| Reopened | 24 June 1995 | |
| | | |
| P&P | No 20 p85, No 46 p91 | |
| Operator | original | EKR |
| | current | EKR |

This is the terminus of the line that once served nearby coal mines, and on which a passenger service was provided. It is adjacent to the main-line station of the same name and is now run as a heritage railway. Prior to closure there were two passenger trains each way on Mondays to Saturdays. There were 12 stations over a mere 11½ miles. Trains currently run most weekends between April and December, with four or five round trips. Most trains are diesel-operated.

Ex-Army diesel locomotive No 427 and motor luggage van No 68001 stand in the single platform on 14 August 2003. This is one of three identical luggage vans on the railway, which were built at Eastleigh in 1959. They are capable of running under battery power.

A view of the platform from the station entrance looking towards the next station of Eythorne. The two passenger coaches form electric unit No 5759, also built at Eastleigh.

## Eythorne                                                                    14,A1

| Opened | | 16 October 1916 |
|---|---|---|
| Closed | | 1 November 1948 |
| Reopened | | 24 June 1995 |
| Operator | original | EKR |
| | current | EKR |

This is the only other station currently open on the EKR and is situated 1¾ miles from Shepherdswell. This attractive wayside station was built by the new railway company, as the original structure had long since been dismantled. The signal box is from Selling on the main line between Canterbury East and Faversham. The road crossing at the north-east end of the station was ungated until services were reinstated.

Both EKR stations have free car parking and other visitor facilities

A view of Eythorne station on 3 October 2006.

Shakespeare Cliff Halt on 9 September 1988.

## Shakespeare Cliff Halt                                                      (14,B1)

| Opened | | 2 June 1913 |
|---|---|---|
| Closed | | see below |
| P&P | | No 46 p86 |
| Operator | original | SECR |
| | current | Network Rail |

This is on the main line between Folkestone and Dover, and was opened for the benefit of miners working at the adjacent colliery (which closed in 1915) and railwaymen who lived nearby. During WWII it was used by military personnel, after which it was dormant for long periods. It was used more recently in relation to the construction of the Channel Tunnel, but then fell into disuse again. It never appeared in public timetables. Because it was, in effect, a private halt, it was never formally closed or reopened.

## Folkestone Harbour                                                                13, B2

| | | |
|---|---|---|
| **Opened** | 1 January 1849; resited 1856 | Following the end of regular passenger services, the station was used occasionally for special trains. In the recent past, the most regular visitor has been the 'Orient Express'. This was normally for berthing the empty stock, prior to collecting passengers at Folkestone West. On some occasions passengers boarded at Folkestone Harbour. By this time the station was in a decrepit state, with one platform abandoned – hardly compatible with a prestigious train, or any passenger train at all! |
| **Closed** | No public services from 29 November 1915 | |
| **Reopened** | 1 March 1919 | |
| **Closed** | No public services from 4 September 1939 | |
| **Reopened** | 1945 | |
| **Closed** | Last regular passenger train ran in December 1991; some trains ran until 2 October 2000; remaining traffic (excursions) ceased from 30 May 2002 | |
| **Reopened** | 28 September 2003 for excursion trains | There is a proposal to redevelop the station area as a marina. Other proposals are to build a museum and memorial to troops who used Folkestone Harbour during both World Wars, and to run a lightweight railbus service to the main line under the name 'Remembrance Line'. |
| **Closed** | Last train 14 March 2009 | |
| **Mothballed until** | 15 March 2010 | |
| **P&P** | No 20 p84, No 46 p44 | |
| **Operator original** | SECR | |
| **current** | Network Rail | |

On 20 May 2004 No 67007 waits for 'Orient Express' passengers, delayed by about 2 hours by a late-running ferry. The steep gradient to the main line is apparent from the end of the platform.

# CHANNEL TUNNEL RAIL LINK (HIGH SPEED 1)

## Folkestone Eurotunnel Shuttle Terminal      13, B2

| | | |
|---|---|---|
| **Terminal opened for HGVs** | 19 May 1994 | Shuttle services run to Coquelles. Cars are normally conveyed in double-deck covered wagons and larger vehicles in single-deck wagons. Passengers are not required to remain in their vehicles. Lorries are conveyed in semi-open wagons and their drivers travel in a coach at the front of the train. |
| **Tunnel opened for freight** | 1 June 1994 | |
| **Tunnel opened for passengers (Eurostar)** | 14 November 1994 | |
| **Terminal opened for cars and occupants** | 22 December 1994 | |
| **Operator**    **original** | Eurotunnel | |
| **current** | Eurotunnel | |

The huge area occupied by the terminal is viewed from Pilgrims' Way, just to the north. Eurostar trains do not call here, but pass by on the southern side of the terminal. One such train is seen between the terminal and the maintenance depot.

Locomotive No 9015 *Lotschberg 1913* leaves with a Shuttle train on 27 May 2004. Another locomotive of the same class is on the rear of the train.

| Sandling | | 13, B2 |
|---|---|---|
| **Opened** | 29 September 2003 | This location is on Section 1 of the Channel Tunnel Rail Link (CTRL), which runs 46 miles to Fawkham Junction, where it connects with Network Rail lines. Construction of this section began in October 1998. |
| **P&P** | No 46 p81 | |
| **Operator** original | Eurostar | |
| **current** | Eurostar | |

A Eurostar train from Waterloo International heads for Brussels on 27 May 2004. The former SECR main line is to the right at a lower level

On the same day, the unusual sight of a Eurostar train on the SECR line.

## Smeeth                                                                (13, B2)

| | | |
|---|---|---|
| **Opened** | October 1852 | This location is adjacent to the site of Smeeth station, where the High Speed line runs parallel to the Network Rail (ex-SECR) line and the M20 motorway as far as Ashford. |
| **Closed** | 4 January 1954 | |
| **Opened (CTRL)** | 28 September 2003 | |
| **P&P** | No 46 p81 | |
| **Operator** original | SECR | |
| **current** | Southeastern and Eurostar on separate lines | |

A Eurostar train seen from the former SECR line on 20 May 2004.

## Ashford International                                                   13, B2

| | | |
|---|---|---|
| **Previous name** | Ashford | Ashford station has been extensively rebuilt for both the traditional and the new Eurostar trains, the latter now using dedicated lines. The High Speed line crosses the Ashford-Canterbury line on a mile-long viaduct. passing round the back of the station, then into a tunnel under the Ashford-Maidstone line. Within the tunnel is the junction for chords serving the station. The High Speed line continues to Maidstone, Rochester and Southfleet, mostly parallel to motorways and trunk roads. At Southfleet, Section 1 turns south to Fawkham Junction, where it joins the Network Rail system. |
| **Opened** | 1 December 1842 | |
| **Extensively rebuilt and enlarged** | 1994 | |
| **Official 'reopening'** | Fully operational from 8 January 1996 | |
| **Opened (CTRL)** | 29 September 2003 | |
| **P&P** | No 46 pp12, 34, 66, 75, 80 | |
| **Operator** original | SECR | |
| **current** | Southeastern and Eurostar | |

*Top:* The viaduct dominates this photograph, taken at the south end of Ashford on 27 May 2004. To the right a Eurostar train from Waterloo to Paris has just called at the station.

*Centre:* This is south of Ashford, looking towards Dover on the same day. The Charing Cross-Dover main line is on the far right.

*Right:* Eurostar unit No 3231 leaves Ashford International with a Paris-Waterloo service on 27 May 2004.

The leading unit of this Paris-Waterloo train at Ashford is No 3002, seen on 3 April 2003, a few months prior to the opening of the High Speed line.

An up Eurostar train approaches Ashford on the Network Rail main line on the same day. In the right background are the former locomotive and carriage works, while on the left is the new High Speed viaduct, not yet in use.

| Southfleet | | (36, C2) |
|---|---|---|
| Opened | 10 May 1886 | |
| Closed | 3 August 1953 | |
| Opened (CTRL Section 1) | 28 September 2003 | |
| Closed (passenger services) | 14 November 2007 | |
| P&P | No 7 p91 | |
| Operator original | SECR | |
| current | Eurostar/Network Rail | |

The CTRL Section 1 line, seen here on 20 March 2003, was built on the trackbed of the Gravesend West branch from Fawkham Junction.

A Eurostar train approaches Southfleet Junction on 21 May 2004, where the lines for Waterloo and St Pancras services diverge. The former line is no longer used by Eurostar or any other passenger trains.

## Ebbsfleet International and                                    38, C2
## Ebbsfleet International Domestic

| | | |
|---|---|---|
| **Originally to be named** | Gravesend International | There is a park-and-ride facility here, giving easy access to the station from the A2 trunk road and M25 motorway. The station has separate platforms for the High Speed international and domestic services. An interim service from St Pancras to Ebbsfleet and Ashford was introduced on 29 June 2009, and services to other destinations in Kent were introduced in December 2009. A spur joins the North Kent (Network Rail) line at Springhead Junction. |
| **Opened** | 19 November 2007 (Eurostar services) 14 December 2009 (full domestic services) | |
| **P&P** | No 46 p121 | |
| **Operator** original | Network Rail | |
| current | Network Rail | |

Ebbsfleet on 13 May 2005, prior to opening. The connection to the North Kent line is on the viaduct, with the platforms in the background. International and domestic platforms for Ashford are side by side.

*Top:* New 'Javelin' High Speed unit No 395012, forming a Dover-St Pancras service, approaches Ebbsfleet on the first day of the full service, 14 December 2009. Domestic trains to and from Dover use the two faces of the Low Level island platform. The other Low Level platforms are segregated for customs and immigration purposes and are used exclusively by Eurostar trains.

*Centre:* Unit No 395019 leaves Ebbsfleet High Level on the same day, forming a service from Faversham.

*Left:* The view from Ebbsfleet High Level looking toward Springhead Junction, where the High Speed line ends and trains join the North Kent line. The train in the background is on a Charing Cross-Gravesend service.

Unit No 395012 from Dover leaves the Low Level station on 14 December 2009. To the immediate right is the Eurostar line. The viaduct further to the right carries the domestic High Speed lines to North Kent.

# SITTINGBOURNE-SHEERNESS-ON-SEA

## Swale                                                                         13, A1

| | | |
|---|---|---|
| **Previous name** | Kings Ferry Bridge Halt | The new station is on a diverted line, replacing a halt of the same name. The station is served by two trains an hour in each direction outside peak periods on Mondays to Saturdays and hourly on Sundays. It was only a few years ago (post-privatisation) that there was an attempt to reduce the service to one train per week. The old alignment and halt lie to the east at a lower level. The line is promoted by SRCP. |
| **Opened** | 1913 as staff halt | |
| **Opened** | December 1922 for public use; formally opened on 1 March 1923 | |
| **Opened on new site** | 10 April 1960 | |
| **P&P** | No 46 p108 | |
| **Operator**          original | SECR | |
|                       current | Southeastern | |

Class 4-CEP EMU (later Class 411) No 1601 pauses at Swale on the shuttle service to Sittingbourne on 1 September 1989.

## Tenterden Town — 13, B1

| | | |
|---|---|---|
| **Previous name** | Tenterden | |
| **Opened** | 15 April 1903 | |
| **Closed** | 4 January 1954; some later special trains | |
| **Reopened** | 3 February 1974 | |
| **P&P** **P&PC** | No 20 p137, No 46 p20; KESR pp33-40 | |
| **Operator** original | KESR | |
| current | KESR | |

The station is conveniently situated for the town. Prior to closure there were three trains a day to Robertsbridge and five to Headcorn, with no Sunday service. The present-day service runs on most weekends throughout the year and on many weekdays outside the winter period.

These two views of the station on 11 August 1987 show the single platform, with carriage sidings and works on the right. The line drops significantly beyond the level crossing toward Rolvenden.

## Rolvenden                                                    13, B1

| Previous name | | Tenterden |
|---|---|---|
| Opened | | 2 April 1900 |
| Closed | | 4 January 1954; some later special trains |
| Reopened | | 3 February 1974 |
| P&P P&PC | | No 46 p21 KESR pp49-65 |
| Operator | original | KESR |
| | current | KESR |

This was the headquarters of the original railway company and is currently where the locomotive shed and works are located. There are typically five trains per day in each direction, the majority being steam-hauled.

*This page and opposite:* Four views of the station taken on 5 June 1996. Wittersham Road station on 5 June 1996.

## Wittersham Road        13, B1

| | | This is an isolated station some distance from Wittersham, as the name implies. It was the terminus in the early years of the reopened line. |
|---|---|---|
| **Opened** | 2 April 1900 | |
| **Closed** | 4 January 1954; some later special trains | |
| **Reopened** | 1978 | |
| **P&PC** | KESR pp66-68 | |
| **Operator** original | KESR | |
| current | KESR | |

The hut in the centre is the booking office, unusually at right-angles to the platform.

To the north of the station is a small yard, used for the storage of rolling stock and materials.

| Northiam | | 13, B1 |
|---|---|---|
| Opened | 2 April 1900 | This is the first of the KESR stations over the border in Sussex. |
| Closed | 4 January 1954; some later special trains | |
| Reopened | 5 June 1996 | |
| P&P P&PC | No 46 p127; KESR pp69-72 | |
| Operator original | KESR | |
| current | KESR | |

On 5 June 1996 the newly constructed platform can be seen on the north side of the line and new trackwork in the process of being installed. The original platform on this side had been demolished many years before.

The main platform and simple building survived and have been carefully restored.

## Bodiam                                                             13, B1

| Opened | 2 April 1900 | Track is being laid west of Bodiam, with a view to extending services towards the original destination of Robertsbridge. This is being pursued by the Rother Valley Railway, which has a site for a new Robertsbridge station to be named Northbridge Street. |
|---|---|---|
| Closed | 4 January 1954; some later special trains | |
| Reopened | 2 April 2000 | |
| P&P P&PC | No 46 p126; KESR pp73-77 | |
| Operator original | KESR | |
| current | KESR | |

The station, seen here on 5 June 1996, was partially restored several years prior to reopening. The small goods yard was used for the storage of wagons.

Further restoration took place just before reopening and the station is currently the western terminus of the line. The date is 30 June 2003.

## Tunbridge Wells West      12, B2

| Previous name | | Tunbridge Wells |
| --- | --- | --- |
| Opened | | 1 October 1866 |
| Closed | | 8 July 1985 |
| Reopened | | 1996 |
| P&P | | No 20 p67, No 46 pp58-60 |
| Operator | original | LBSCR |
| | current | SVR |

Tunbridge Wells West was a grand station, but all that remains for railway purposes is a single new platform and the original locomotive depot.

Two views of the Spa Valley Railway's station on 23 July 2004. In the second picture, the old station building is in the background and forms part of a shopping centre.

## High Rocks                                                                12, B2

| Previous name | | High Rocks Halt |
|---|---|---|
| Opened | | 1 June 1907 |
| Closed | | 16 October 1939 |
| Reopened | | 15 June 1942 |
| Closed | | 5 May 1952 |
| Reopened | | August 1998 |
| Operator | original | LBSCR |
| | current | SVR |

Building of the new High Rocks was funded by the owner of the adjacent inn of the same name, which is accessible directly from the single platform. The original halt had two platforms, as there were separate up and down lines

The Spa Valley Railway's High Rocks station on 23 July 2004.

## Groombridge                                                      12, B2

| Opened | 1 October 1866 | In BR steam days Groombridge had four trains per hour every day of the week in each direction, serving Brighton, Eastbourne, East Grinstead and London, with additional trains during the morning and evening peak periods. Trains currently run most weekends throughout the year, with typically five departures per day. |
|---|---|---|
| Closed | 8 July 1985 | |
| Reopened | August 1997, resited | |
| P&P | No 45 pp94-96 | |
| Operator  original | LBSCR | |
| current | SVR | |

Groombridge station has been relocated, as the original station and adjoining land had been sold in the intervening period. The old station has been tastefully restored and is used by a small business. Groombridge is currently the western terminus of the Spa Valley Railway. The old station is immediately beyond the bridge in this 23 July 2004 view.

Another view of the station, looking towards Eridge on 5 June 2003. It is anticipated that the service will be extended to Eridge in the near future.

## Birchden (Groombridge-Eridge spur)                                   12, B2

| | | |
|---|---|---|
| Opened | 3 August 1868 | The spur was used by trains running between Tunbridge Wells and the South Coast, and it joined the Oxted-Eridge line at Birchden Junction. The latter line is still open as far as Uckfield; the Uckfield trains, operated by Southern, use the old up line. The junction itself no longer exists and Spa Valley Railway trains will run on the old down line from Birchden Junction to Eridge. |
| Closed | 6 July 1985 | |
| Reopened | expected April 2011 | |
| P&P | No 20 p69, No 45 p81 | |
| Operator original | LBSCR | |
| current | SVR | |

*Left:* Class 'D1' No 31492 has just negotiated Birchden Junction with the 11.55am train from Brighton to Tonbridge on 16 March 1958. The line to Oxted is in the foreground.

*Right:* DMU No 207015 passes Birchden Junction signal box forming an Oxted to Uckfield train 30 years later on 6 May 1988. By this time the junction pointwork had been disconnected.

# LEWES-EAST GRINSTEAD

## Newick & Chailey                                                   (12, C1)

| | |
|---|---|
| Opened | 1 August 1882 |
| Closed | No trains from 30 May 1955; formally closed 13 June 1955 |
| Reopened | 7 August 1956 |
| Closed | 17 March 1958 |
| P&P / P&PC | No 45 p55 / BluR pp82-84 |
| Operator original | LBSCR |
| last | BR(S) |

There was a passing loop here and two platforms, but the up platform had been out of use for many years before closure.

This photograph was taken on 30 May 1955 during a rail strike, after the last train had run but prior to the formal closing date.

| Sheffield Park | | 12, B1 |
|---|---|---|
| **Previous name** | Fletching & Sheffield Park | Sheffield Park is currently the headquarters of the Bluebell Railway. |
| **Opened** | 1 August 1882 | |
| **Closed** | No trains from 30 May 1955; formally closed 13 June 1955 | |
| **Reopened** | 7 August 1956 | |
| **Closed** | 17 March 1958 | |
| **Reopened** | 31 July 1960 | |
| **P&P** **P&PC** | No 20 pp140-141, No 45 p56; BluR pp72-80 | |
| **Operator**          original | LBSCR | |
|          current | BluR | |

Facilities were basic and trains were short in the early years following reopening. On 25 May 1966 ex-LBSCR Class 'A1X' No 72, painted in the livery of the Newhaven Harbour Company, waits to leave for Bluebell Halt (then the northern terminus of the line), with an ex-LNWR observation coach and an SECR 3rd Class 'birdcage' brake-van.

BR Class 4MT No 80064 approaches Sheffield Park with a train of main-line Maunsell SR corridor coaches from Horsted Keynes on 24 October 1987.

## Ketche's Halt (12, B1)

| | | This is the most southerly of four halts on the Bluebell Railway, but was the only one not to be served on a regular basis. It was also the only halt without road access. It was named after the nearby farm and was the last halt to open, which took place after the others had been closed. |
|---|---|---|
| **Opened** | 29 May 1989 | |
| **Closed** | Fell into disuse | |
| **Operator original** | BluR | |
| **last** | BluR | |

Ketche's Halt on 22 March 2009. *Martin Lawrence*

## Freshfield Halt (12, B1)

| | | This isolated halt had access from a country road that passed under the railway immediately north of the station. |
|---|---|---|
| **Opened** | 1 August 1960 | |
| **Closed** | 19 April 1989 | |
| **P&P** **P&PC** | No 18 p130; BluR pp57, 58 | |
| **Operator original** | BluR | |
| **last** | BluR | |

A train heading for Sheffield Park on 15 July 1961 is hauled by SECR Class 'P' No 323 *Bluebell*, while on the rear is LSWR Class '0415' No 488. An engine was required at both ends, as there was at the time no access to run-round facilities at Horsted Keynes.

## Holywell (Waterworks) Halt                                        (12, B1)

| Opened | | 1 August 1960 |
|---|---|---|
| Closed | | 31 October 1963 |
| P&P | | No 18 p129 |
| Operator | original | BluR |
| | last | BluR |

The halt was marginally closer to Horsted Keynes village than is Horsted Keynes station.

On 31 July 1962 a train for Sheffield Park passes the halt, hauled by Class 'A1X' No 55 *Stepney*. On the rear is Class 'P' No 27.

## Bluebell Halt                                                     (12, B1)

| Opened | | 1 August 1960 |
|---|---|---|
| Closed | | March 1968 |
| P&P  P&PC | | No 18 p128  BluR p128 |
| Operator | original | BluR |
| | last | BluR |

This was a temporary halt, which acted as the northern terminus of the line until access to Horsted Keynes was granted. Horsted Keynes never closed, as it had an electric train service from Seaford and Haywards Heath. Bluebell trains were allowed to use the BR station before the electric service was withdrawn.

The corridor coach on the extreme right was not part of the train, but was used as Bluebell Halt's booking office. The date is 15 July 1961.

## West Hoathly                                                (12, B1)

| | | West Hoathly was demolished following the second closure and permission has not been granted for its reinstatement. When Bluebell Railway services were first extended beyond Horsted Keynes trains ran to New Coombe Bridge, immediately north of West Hoathly, but passengers were not able to join or alight. There are plans for a station to be built at New Coombe Bridge, but these are unlikely to be pursued until after the Bluebell Railway reaches East Grinstead. |
|---|---|---|
| **Opened** | 1 August 1882 | |
| **Closed** | No trains from 30 May 1955; formally closed 13 June 1955 | |
| **Reopened** | 7 August 1956 | |
| **Closed** | 17 March 1958 | |
| **P&P** **P&PC** | No 18 p125, No 45 pp57-59; BluR pp30-32 | |
| **Operator    original** | LBSCR | |
| **last** | BR(S) | |

West Hoathly, seen here on 30 May 1955, the date that trains first ceased, was a typical LBSCR country station, serving the villages of West Hoathly and Sharpthorne.

The service run by BR during the second open period usually consisted of a single coach, on 18 February 1958 hauled by BR Class 4MT No 80150.

| Kingscote | | 12, B1 |
|---|---|---|
| **Previous name** | Kingscote for Turner's Hill | Unlike West Hoathly, this station did not reopen between 1956 and 1958. Following first closure the down platform was demolished, but the up platform with its main building remained intact. |
| **Opened** | 1 August 1882 | |
| **Closed** | No trains from 30 May 1955; formally closed 13 June 1955 | |
| **Reopened** | 23 April 1994 | |
| **P&P** **P&PC** | No 18 p124; BluR pp21-29 | |
| **Operator** original | LBSCR | |
| current | BluR | |

SR Class 'Q1' No C1 has arrived from Horsted Keynes with a train of Bulleid coaches on 22 July 1996. Reinstatement of the down platform is in progress.

Work is still in hand several months later, on 18 October 1996. In the platform is BR Mark 1 Brake Composite Corridor coach No 21271, now in use as engineers' vehicle No 977109. The leading wagon is one of several BR ballast hoppers, which were code-named 'Dogfish'.

| East Grinstead | | 12, B1 |
|---|---|---|
| **Previous name** | East Grinstead Low Level | The former Low Level station is currently the terminus for trains from London and Oxted. The High Level station was demolished following closure of the line between Groombridge and Three Bridges. The Oxted-East Grinstead line is promoted by SCRP. There is a shuttle service only. on the Bluebell Railway |
| **Opened** | 1 August 1882 | |
| **Closed** | Dormant from 17 March 1958 | |
| **Reopened** | In regular use from 2 January 1967 following closure of Three Bridges-Tunbridge Wells line | |
| **Opened (Bluebell Railway)** | 5 September 2010 | |
| **P&P** **P&PC** | No 18 pp119-121, No 45 pp60-61; BluR pp11-18 | |
| **Operator** original | LBSCR | |
| current | Southern/BluR | |

Diesel unit No 1117 has just arrived in the down platform from Victoria on 1 May 1986. The line has since been electrified. The former up platform (on the right) is only used during peak periods.

On the same day diesel unit No 1317 enters the station from the south in preparation for the Oxted service.

## Winnersh Triangle                                    11,A1

| Opened | 12 May 1986 | Funding was provided by BR, the County Council and the developer of the adjacent offices and houses. The station has a half-hourly service to Waterloo every day of the week. Gatwick Airport-Reading diesel units pass through the station, but do not stop. |
|---|---|---|
| Operator original | BR(S) | |
| current | SWT | |

LINK LINE

**INTRODUCING YOUR NEW STATION**

The **NEW** WINNERSH TRIANGLE STATION

Opened on the 12th May, this new station is 48 minutes from Guildford and only 9 minutes from Reading.

The train service is hourly Mondays to Saturdays with a two hourly service on Sundays increasing to hourly on Sunday evenings.

At Guildford, there are good connections into the fast Reading—Gatwick Airport service, giving for example, a journey time of 1 hour 45 minutes to Gatwick, and into the Waterloo—Portsmouth and Isle of Wight services.

At Reading there are excellent connections to Bristol, South Wales and the West Country. The station car park has 130 spaces.

**We're getting there** ⇌

On 13 March 2009 EMU No 8028 enters the station forming a Reading-Waterloo service. This is one of 30 units of Class 458, known as 'Junipers'.

## Martins Heron                                                    11,A1

| Opened | 3 October 1988 |
|---|---|
| P&P | No 21 p96 |
| Operator    original | NSE |
| current | SWT |

This is a pleasant brick-built station adjacent to a retail park and housing. Construction costs were met by BR and the County Council. There are half-hourly services to Waterloo and Reading and several freight trains pass though each day.

On 13 March 2009 one of several daily empty stone trains heads for Whatley Quarry behind a Class 59 in Hanson livery.

## Reading Green Park                                              11,A1

| Opening | 2011 |
|---|---|
| Operator | FGW |

This station is being built to serve the nearby business park and stadium. It is close to the M4 motorway and will have a 'park and ride' facility, with a bus service to Reading town. A frequent service will be provided by the Reading-Basingstoke trains.

This is the site of Reading Green Park station, looking towards Reading on 4 May 2010.

## Newbury Racecourse                                                    10, A2

| Opened for race traffic only | 26 September 1905 | This is another station that was built specifically for race traffic, and only opened for regular passenger services in recent times. It has an hourly service of trains from Reading to Newbury on Monday to Saturday and bi-hourly on Sundays. |
|---|---|---|
| Opened for regular service | 16 May 1988 | |
| P&P | No 21 p120 | |
| Operator          original | GWR | |
| current | FGW | |

On 27 June 2009 DMU No 166218 leaves the station for the short journey to Newbury.

Expresses to the West of England pass through the station. On the same day a Class 43 heads the 12.06 Paddington to Penzance service, the first stop after Reading being Exeter St David's.

## Medstead & Four Marks 10, B2

| Previous name | | Medstead |
| --- | --- | --- |
| Opened | | August 1868 |
| Closed | | 5 February 1973 |
| Reopened | | 28 May 1983 |
| P&P | | No 21 p32 |
| Operator | original | LSWR |
| | current | MHR |

This is a beautifully restored station in the style of the latter days of the SR. The signal box is from Wilton South, as the original was demolished after the line was closed by BR. Trains run from Alton every weekend of the year and most weekdays, except in the winter. The standard timetable advertises six trains per day.

The restored station at Medstead & Four Marks on 23 May 2009.

A train from Alresford enters the station behind GWR Class '4200' No 5224.

Trains regularly pass here and on 23 May 2009 'West Country' Class No 34007 *Wadebridge* enters the loop with a train from Alton. The train from Alresford is hauled by the GWR engine.

This general view of the station from the west end shows the recently installed footbridge. The centre span came from Cowes and the other components were newly manufactured.

## Ropley                                                    10, B2

| Opened | | 2 October 1865 |
|---|---|---|
| Closed | | 5 February 1973 |
| Reopened | | 30 April 1977 |
| P&P | | No 21 p33 |
| Operator | original | LSWR |
| | current | MHR |

The outside of the station is not very attractive, but this is compensated by the railway side, which has been restored to depict the early BR period. There is also an excellent picnic and viewing area on the north side of the station.

This is the view from the down platform on 23 May 2009, showing the signal box; as at Medstead & Four Marks, it has come from elsewhere, in this instance Netley.

Ropley is another passing place. The locomotive and carriage works are to the right beyond the approaching train. Visitors are able to watch activities in the works from a viewing area.

## Alresford                                                    10, B2

| Opened | | 2 October 1865 |
|---|---|---|
| Closed | | 5 February 1973 |
| Reopened | | 30 April 1977 |
| P&P | | No 21 p34 |
| Operator | original | LSWR |
| | current | MHR |

This is the western terminus of the line and is another tastefully restored station, in the pre-war SR style. The station is close to the town centre. The former goods shed houses a gift shop and a meeting room.

This 23 May 2009 view of the station is looking toward the end of the line. There are storage sidings beyond the footbridge.

The line was diesel-operated in its final BR years and this 21st-century photograph of 'Hampshire' Class unit No 1125 beautifully recreates the old order.

## Winchester Chesil (10, B2)

| Previous names | Winchester Cheesehill Street, Winchester Cheesehill |
| --- | --- |
| Opened | 4 May 1885 |
| Closed | 4 August 1942 |
| Reopened | 8 March 1943 |
| Closed | 7 March 1960 |
| Reopened | 18 June 1960 |
| Closed | 10 September 1960 |
| Reopened | 17 June 1961 |
| Closed | 9 September 1961 |
| P&P | No 21 pp142, 143 |
| Operator original | GWR |
| at final closure | BR(S) |

This cramped station on the eastern edge of the city was part of the Didcot, Newbury & Southampton Railway. In BR days services were sparse, with only five trains each way on weekdays and none on Sundays. The second and third reopenings were to provide a Saturday-only service to Southampton Terminus, to relieve pressure at Winchester City station. During this period no service was provided north of Chesil.

The station on 22 May 1960, during its second, three-month, closure period.

Prior to the line from here to Shawford Junction closing completely, there was the occasional special train. On 6 September 1964 Class 3MT No 82029 arrives with empty stock to form a special train to Andover and Ludgershall.

| Hedge End | | 10, C2 |
|---|---|---|
| Preview service | 6 May 1990 in connection with Solent Gala | This station was built shortly after the line between Eastleigh and Fareham was electrified and serves new housing development. It was funded by BR and Eastleigh Borough Council. |
| Opened | 14 May 1990 | |
| Operator original | NSE | |
| current | SWT | |

Electric unit No 3479 (Class VEP, later Class 423) passes through the station on 5 May 1990, a few days before its opening, forming a Portsmouth Harbour-Eastleigh service.

Bottom: The current service consists of an hourly train each way between Waterloo and Portsmouth Harbour every day of the week. This view is dated 31 December 1998.

## Southampton Airport Parkway                                    10, C2

| Previous names | Atlantic Park Hostel Halt, Southampton Airport, Southampton Parkway |
| --- | --- |
| Opened | 30 October 1929 |
| Closed | No records found |
| Reopened | 1 April 1966 |
| Rebuilt and 'reopened' | 29 September 1986 |
| P&P | No 21 p57 |
| Operator    original | NSE |
| current | SWT |

The first station on this site had only a down platform, giving access to the nearby immigration camp. It was not in the public timetable and closed after only a few years. The next station was built for airport passengers. Following the opening of the nearby motorway its remit was expanded and a significantly enhanced train service introduced. It is currently served by two trains per hour between Waterloo and Weymouth, hourly Reading to Brockenhurst, hourly from Salisbury and Cross Country trains between Manchester and Bournemouth. Even on Sundays the station has four trains per hour in each direction.

A 'Wessex Electric' unit (Class 442) works a Weymouth-Waterloo service on 19 April 1993. These units are no longer operated by SWT and most are used on Gatwick expresses.

Outer-suburban unit No 450569 from Waterloo heads for Poole on 23 May 2009. The extensive car park is situated on the right (up) side, adjacent to the railway. Modifications to the station building have taken place since the earlier photograph was taken.

Express electric unit No 444045 forms a Weymouth to Waterloo train on the same day.

## Chandlers Ford                                                    10, C1

| Opened | 1 March 1847 |
|---|---|
| Closed | 5 May 1969 |
| Reopened | 18 May 2003 |
| Operator    original | LSWR |
| current | SWT |

The station was closed due to lack of use and the line between Eastleigh and Romsey became freight-only, the buildings were demolished and the line singled. With the expansion of housing to the west of Eastleigh, the need to reopen the station became apparent. The new station is on the site of the original Romsey-bound platform. On reopening, trains ran only between Romsey and Totton, but they now run half-hourly on all days of the week from Salisbury, via Romsey, Southampton Central, Southampton Parkway and Eastleigh, then back to Romsey, where they terminate. The line is still also used regularly by freight trains. Stations in this area are promoted by the Three Rivers Community Rail Partnership.

The exterior of this pleasant and functional station. The footbridge does not lead to another platform, but to houses on the north side of the line.

The line is hemmed in at the Eastleigh end of the station, as demonstrated by diesel unit No 170304 on a Romsey to Totton service on 24 May 2004.

Class 66 No 66005 takes a train of oil wagons from Fawley to Plymouth on the same day.

The service to Totton was operated exclusively by Class 170s, in this instance No 170392.

## Hardley Halt                                                                                    (10, C2)

| | |
|---|---|
| **Opened** | 3 March 1958 |
| **Closed** | 5 April 1965 |
| **Operator** original | BR(S) |
| last | BR(S) |

The halt was situated 1 mile from the end of the line at Fawley, which is now freight-only. It did not appear in the public timetable and was provided for workers in the refinery industry.

The recently opened Hardley Halt on 17 May 1958. *Hugh Davies/'Photos from the Fifties'*

## Ampress                                                                                         (6, A1)

| | |
|---|---|
| **Previous name** | Ampress Works Halt |
| **Opened** | 1 October 1956 |
| **Closed** | 6 October 1989 |
| **P&P** | No 21 p88 |
| **Operator** original | BR(S) |
| last | NSE |

The station is situated on the Lymington branch and trains from Brockenhurst pass through very frequently. However, it did not appear in the public timetable, and was built for workers at an adjacent factory, which has since closed. The site has been redeveloped for a hospital, which opened in 2007, and there is also a business park nearby. There is some discussion about reopening, but access is difficult, as the station is on a high embankment.

The notice on the platform in this 18 March 1993 view declares that Ampress is in the 'Open Station system', but it is not clear from the photograph how passengers are expected to reach the platform.

As seen on 9 April 2004, the platform is still in situ.

## Smallbrook Junction    6, A2

| Opened | 21 July 1991 |
|---|---|
| P&P | No 51 pp103-105 |
| Operator original | NSE and IWSR |
| current | Island Line/IWSR |

This is an interchange station only and there is no public access, other than by train. 'Island Line' trains only stop when there is a service on the IWSR.

A former London Underground train, now Class 483 No 006, has just left the station forming a service from Shanklin to Ryde Pier Head on 5 May 2004.

The Isle of Wight Steam Railway platform is at a higher level, on the right-hand side.

Unit No 002 *Raptor* picks up passengers for Ryde from the last steam train working of the day.

Unit No 004 makes a special stop for the photographer, who was heading south.

## Ashey 6, A2

| | | |
|---|---|---|
| **Previous name** | Ashey for Nunwell | |
| **Opened** | 20 December 1875 | |
| **Closed** | 21 February 1966 | |
| **Reopened** | 2 May 1993 | |
| **P&P** | No 51 pp65-67 | |
| **Operator** original | IWCR | |
| current | IWSR | |

This single-platform station is in most attractive surroundings. There is no public road access, although there is a public footpath. Trains only call on request.

The house on the right was at one time the main station building and is now in private hands.

LBSCR Class 'A1X' No 8 *Freshwater* approaches Ashey from Smallbrook Junction with a train of coaches from the same era on 5 May 2004.

## Havenstreet                                                      6, A2

| Previous name | Haven Street |
|---|---|
| Opened | June 1876 (line opened 20 December 1875) |
| Closed | 21 February 1966 |
| Reopened | 31 May 1971 |
| P&P | No 51 pp55-64 |
| Operator original | IWCR |
| current | IWSR |

This island-platform station was used as a crossing point for trains in BR and earlier days. It has been splendidly restored and now forms part of the headquarters of the IWSR. There is a shop, refreshment rooms, a museum, carriage, wagon and locomotive works, and storage sidings.

On 5 May 2004, passengers watch as No 8 comes off shed, prior to working a train to Smallbrook Junction, waiting on the left.

All trains are formed of former BR-owned coaches used on the Island until closure. Most are of LBSCR origin, but much rebuilt by previous owners and refurbished by the present railway company. The water tower originally stood at Newport.

| Wootton | | 6, A2 |
| --- | --- | --- |
| Opened | 1876 (line opened 20 December 1875) | Wootton sees between four and six trains during summer, with fewer out of the main season. The signal box came from Freshwater, which closed in 1953; it then saw use as a bus shelter, before being acquired by the IWSR. |
| Closed | 21 September 1953 | |
| Reopened | 7 August 1986 on new site | |
| P&P | No 51 pp53, 54 | |
| Operator original | IWCR | |
| current | IWSR | |

Wootton, seen here on 5 May 2004, is the terminus of the present-day Isle of Wight Steam Railway.

Passengers board a train for Smallbrook Junction on 26 May 2004, hauled by No 198 Royal Engineer.

## Lake                                              6, A2

| Previous name | | Lake Halt |
|---|---|---|
| Opened | | 1904 |
| Closed | | No record found |
| Reopened | | 11 May 1987 |
| P&P | | No 51 p77 |
| Operator | original | IWR |
| | current | Island Line |

Little is known about the original halt, believed to have been near the present station. It was apparently used mainly by passengers to the nearby cricket ground, and is thought to have been out of use only a few years after opening. This and other stations on the island are promoted by the IWCRP.

Class 486 No 032, a former Underground train built in the 1930s, approaches Lake with a Shanklin service on 14 August 1987.

There is a single, narrow, wooden platform, well placed in a residential area with many guesthouses for holidaymakers.

## Swanage        5, A2

| Opened | 20 May 1885 |
|---|---|
| Closed | 3 January 1972 |
| Reopened | 29 March 1987 |
| P&P | No 29 p68, No 44 pp75-77 |
| Operator  original | LSWR |
| current | SwanR |

Swanage has been transformed over the past few years and is once again a thriving station with a good service operated by steam and diesel trains on every weekend throughout the year. There are also trains most weekdays from April to October, with typically six departures per day. The maximum in high summer is 17 per day.

Classic views of Swanage station on 13 September 1986, in the early years when the line was only open as far as Herston. The engine is an 0-6-0 saddle tank named *Linda*, from the Corby Iron & Steel Works.

It is now commonplace to see Bulleid 'Pacifics' hauling long trains out of Swanage, in this case No 34028 *Eddystone* on 10 April 2004. The Class 108 diesel unit was often seen on evening trains and at less busy periods. It is currently undergoing renovation.

Passengers await the arrival of a train from Norden on the same day, hauled by LSWR Class 'M7' No 30053. This engine used to operate on the Swanage line in BR days.

## Herston Halt 5,A2

| Opened | April 1984 | Since becoming a through station, the halt has been a request stop, and is used by walkers and people from the local camp sites. It was rebuilt over the winter of 2008/09 and officially reopened on 30 May 2009. |
|---|---|---|
| Operator original | SwanR | |
| current | SwanR | |

Herston Halt on 13 December 2005. In the adjacent siding is an SR covered carriage truck (No S 4594) and some engineers' vehicles.

## Harmans Cross 5,A2

| Opened | March 1989 | This is a new location for a station, which provides access to the village of the same name, the Purbeck countryside and nearby campsites. The Swanage Railway has beautifully created a typical SR scene, with lamp posts complete with 'target' station name plates and buildings in the traditional style. |
|---|---|---|
| Operator original | SwanR | |
| current | SwanR | |

Class 'M7' No 30053 takes an afternoon train from Norden to Swanage on 10 April 2004.

Harmans Cross is used as a crossing point for up and down trains when there is a frequent service in operation,
as was the case on 10 April 2004.

## Corfe Castle                                                                  5, A2

| Opened | 20 May 1885 | The station is ideally placed and is well patronised by local people and the many tourists who come to see the castle and village. |
|---|---|---|
| Closed | 3 January 1972 | |
| Reopened | April 1995 | |
| P&P | No 29 p65, No 44 pp73, 74 | |
| Operator original | LSWR | |
| current | SwanR | |

A train approaching the station from Swanage on 28 October 2008 is about to enter the up loop. Some of the vans on the right have been restored and form part of a small and interesting museum.

In addition to basic restoration of the station prior to the reintroduction of train services, two major events have taken place in more recent years, first the reinstatement of the down platform, followed by the installation of a footbridge, which came from Merton Park and was erected in 2007.

## Norden                                                                5,A2

| Opened | | 12 August 1995 | Norden is situated just to the north of Corfe Castle and offers a park-and-ride facility. This is well used, as it is far easier to take the train to Swanage than to drive, particularly during summer holidays. |
|---|---|---|---|
| Operator | original | SwanR | |
| | current | SwanR | |

The 'M7' prepares to leave with a morning train to Swanage on 10 April 2004. The large car park is just out of sight to the right. There is also a refreshment bar, picnic and play areas.

Adjacent sidings and those beyond the station are used for storing rolling stock awaiting renovation.

Looking towards Corfe Castle from the single platform at Norden on 28 October 2008, to the right is one of two Class 33 diesels on the railway, and several engineers' vehicles. Close by is the Purbeck Mineral & Mining Museum.

The hut in the centre of the platform is the booking office. The refreshment bar is just off the platform on an embankment by the side of the line.

| Furzebrook | | 5,A2 |
|---|---|---|
| Opened | 20 May 1885 | The railhead for oil and gas from Wytch Farm was located at Furzebrook and opened in 1978. Cessation of this traffic in May 2005 has given the opportunity for the Swanage Railway to pursue plans for running a regular service to Wareham, on the main line from Waterloo to Weymouth. |
| Closed to passenger trains | 3 January 1972 | |
| Reopened | 8 August 2002, April and May 2009; temporary openings to passenger trains | |
| Opened for regular service | anticipated 2013 | |
| Operator          original | LSWR | |
| current | Network Rail | |

Locomotive No 66198 brings a train of empty tank wagons from Eastleigh into Furzebrook on 20 April 2004.

The same locomotive runs round its train prior to propelling it into the depot.

## Weymouth Tramway and Quay                                             5, A1

| Station names | Weymouth Landing Stage, Weymouth Quay |
|---|---|
| Line opened | 16 October 1865 |
| Station opened | 4 August 1889 |
| Closed | 25 July 1940 to regular passenger services |
| Reopened | 15 June 1946 to regular passenger services |
| Closed | Last regular passenger train from Waterloo 26 September 1987; specials until 30 May 1999 |
| P&P | No 29 pp4, 124-130, No 44 pp51-54 |
| Operator original | GWR |
| current | Network Rail |

In its heyday the line saw several boat trains per day in the summer, the majority from Paddington. However, from 1959 all trains ran to and from Waterloo. So few trains were run in later years that it was commonplace for motorists to park across the track. The tramway is currently out of use, despite several attempts to reinstate it for occasional special trains.

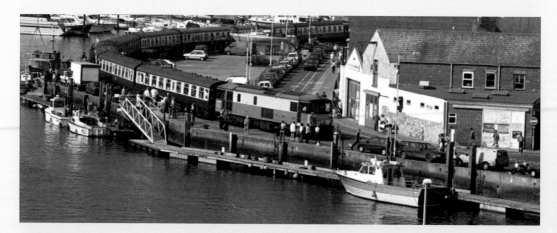

The difficulties of running trains on this line can be seen as electro-diesel No 73138 inches its way toward the Quay on 2 May 1999.

On an earlier occasion, 6 April 1995, No 37407 *Blackpool Tower* runs round its train at Quay station, in preparation for the return journey along the Southern main line.

## Cranmore 9, B1

| Opened | 9 November 1858 |
|---|---|
| Closed | 9 September 1963 |
| Reopened | 1985 |
| P&P | No 30 p70 |
| Operator original | GWR |
| current | ESR |

The site was purchased from BR by the artist David Shepherd OBE in 1972 and was opened to the public the following year. Train services from Cranmore were not provided until 1985. Trains operate at weekends between April and December, as well as on weekdays in midsummer. There are between four and eight trains per day, almost always steam-hauled.

Diesel shunter No 45 brings empty stock for a train to Mendip Vale on 3 June 2009. This locomotive once belonged to the Merseyside Docks & Harbour Board.

The station complex at Cranmore, including a restaurant, art gallery, museum and shop, was built in 1991, when the platform was also extended. There is a large car park and picnic area.

| Cranmore West Platform | | | 9, B1 |
|---|---|---|---|
| Opened | | 1978 | Until the opening of Cranmore station, this was the starting point for passenger trains. |
| Operator | original | ESR | |
| | current | ESR | |

The platform, seen here on 3 June 2009, was built from material salvaged from Ilton Halt, between Chard and Taunton.

To the left of the station is the locomotive depot and works, both built in 1973; a public viewing gallery is provided. In the distance is Cranmore station.

## Merryfield Lane Halt                                                      9, B1

| Opened | | 1981 |
| --- | --- | --- |
| Operator | original | ESR |
| | current | ESR |

The halt, where a picnic area is provided, is at the summit of the line, and was the terminus until the extension to Mendip Vale was built four years later.

The only access to the halt, photographed on 3 June 2009, is by train.

Prior to the opening of the extension, the siding was part of the run-round loop.

| Mendip Vale | | | 9, B1 |
|---|---|---|---|
| Opened | | 1993 | Trains ran to Mendip Vale from 1985, but it was not possible to alight or join trains here for another eight years. The line used to continue to Shepton Mallet, but Mendip Vale is now the terminus. |
| Operator | original | ESR | |
| | current | ESR | |

There is no road access to Mendip Vale, but the station can be reached by public footpath.
These pictures are dated 3 June 2009.

# BRISTOL–EXETER (GREAT WESTERN MAIN LINE)

## Worle
8, A1

| Previous names | Banwell, Puxton & Worle |
|---|---|
| **Main-line station:** | |
| Opened | 14 June 1841 |
| Closed | 6 April 1964 |
| Reopened | 24 September 1990 on new site |
| **Loop station:** | |
| Opened | 1 March 1884 |
| Closed | 1 January 1922 |
| Operator   original | GWR |
| current | FGW |

There were two previous stations, one on the main line and the other on the Weston-super-Mare loop. The current station at St George's is nearer to the site of the original main-line station, and was built to serve the nearby business park and residential area. On the direction signs from the M5 motorway, it is referred to as Worle Parkway. It has two trains each way per hour, and there are also frequent non-stop trains from Birmingham and Paddington to South Devon and Cornwall.

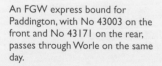

Diesel unit No 150249 calls with a Bristol Temple Meads to Taunton service on 19 August 2007.

An FGW express bound for Paddington, with No 43003 on the front and No 43171 on the rear, passes through Worle on the same day.

## Tiverton Parkway                                                                7, C2

| Previous names | Sampford Peverell, Sampford Peverell Halt |
|---|---|
| Opened | 9 July 1928 |
| Closed | 5 October 1964 |
| Reopened | 12 May 1986 |
| P&P | No 8 pp9, 10, No 52 p106 |
| Operator  original | GWR |
| current | FGW |

The new station was built on the site of Sampford Peverell Halt. Tiverton Junction station, which was nearly 2 miles to the south, was closed in May 1986 when the Parkway station was built for commuters from the M5 motorway and the North Devon Link Road. Some of the latter road was built on the formation of the Tiverton to Barnstaple line.

Tiverton Parkway, photographed on 29 October 2008.

## Norton Fitzwarren (8, B1)

| | | |
|---|---|---|
| **Opened** | 1873 (2 October?) | |
| **Closed** | 30 October 1961 | |
| **Reopened** | 1 August 2009 on new site | |
| **P&P** | No 30 pp136, 137 | |
| **Operator** original | GWR | |
| current | WSR | |

The station was originally on the GWR main line at the junction for the Minehead branch. The new station is on the branch a short distance from the site of the junction. There is currently no regular passenger service and no public access to the station.

The first train on the first day of operations, 1 August 2009, arrived from Minehead in torrential rain. A first day platform ticket.

For the remainder of the day the unit, comprising coaches from BR units of Classes 115 and 117, ran a shuttle service to Bishops Lydeard.

## Bishops Lydeard                                                    8, B1

| | | |
|---|---|---|
| **Opened** | 31 March 1862 | This is the starting point for the vast majority of passengers travelling on the line to Minehead. There are between four and eight departures per day between April and October; for the remainder of the year, a service is only provided on a few days per week. Most trains are steam-hauled. |
| **Closed** | 4 January 1971 | |
| **Reopened** | 9 June 1979 | |
| **P&P** **P&PC** | No 30 pp138, 139 WSR pp21-28; WSR(2) pp18-26 | |
| **Operator original** | GWR | |
| **current** | WSR | |

Attention to detail is a hallmark of the WSR, as exemplified by these two illustrations taken on 9 June 2009, the 30th anniversary of the reopening of the station.

Activity at Bishops Lydeard in preparation for the start of the day's services on 9 June 2009. In the bay is No 9351, rebuilt from GWR Class '5100' No 5193, with the addition of a tender; it entered service in 2004. The diesel shunter is Class 08 No D3462, and on the far right is Class '5100' No 4160.

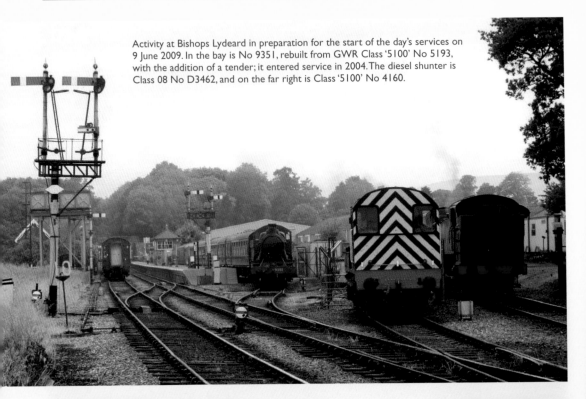

No 4160 passes under the bridge at the north end of the station on the first train of the day to Minehead.

| Crowcombe Heathfield | | 8, B1 |
|---|---|---|
| **Previous name** | Crowcombe | The WSR took over a desolate station with no signal box and overgrown platforms, and it is now a beautifully restored station in attractive surroundings. Trains pass here in peak periods. |
| **Opened** | 31 March 1862 | |
| **Closed** | 4 January 1971 | |
| **Reopened** | 9 June 1979 | |
| **P&P** **P&PC** | No 30 p140 WSR pp29-32; P&PC WSR(2) pp27-32 | |
| **Operator    original** | GWR | |
| **current** | WSR | |

Class '2800' No 3850 carefully enters the station with a train to Bishops Lydeard on 10 June 2009.

The transformation that has taken place since the WSR took over the station is amazing, with new or refurbished buildings, and well-maintained and tidy platforms.

## Stogumber                                                                7, B2

| Opened | 31 March 1862 |
| --- | --- |
| Closed | 4 January 1971 |
| Reopened | 7 May 1978 |
| P&P<br>P&PC | No 30 p6<br>WSR pp33-37; WSR(2) pp36-38 |
| Operator    original | GWR |
| current | WSR |

The station is approached by road on a steep hill, and is located on a ledge, with a steep drop on the west side, about a mile beyond which is Stogumber village. The original platform was wooden, and was rebuilt and the platform lengthened at the end of the 20th century. The waiting shelter was replaced in 2009.

The brick base on the right is the remains of the cattle dock. Beyond this is the original station building, still in use.

The view from the Minehead end of the station on 10 June 2009, with a morning train in the hands of No 3850.

| Williton | | 7, B2 |
|---|---|---|
| Opened | 31 March 1862 | Trains pass here throughout the season. The station is situated at the eastern extremity of the village, and also features a maintenance and restoration centre for diesel locomotives, under the auspices of the Diesel & Electric Preservation Group. |
| Closed | 4 January 1971 | |
| Reopened | 28 August 1976 | |
| P&P P&PC | No 30 p141 WSR pp38-44; WSR(2) pp40-47 | |
| Operator  original | GWR | |
| current | WSR | |

The Diesel & Electric Preservation Group's centre is situated on the down side of the line at the far end of the station, where the retreating train can be seen on 9 June 2009. The train in the foreground is hauled by No 3850, and to the right in the siding is SR PMV No S 1458.

The last train of the day disappears round the curve towards Stogumber on 10 June 2009. The bridge carries the road from Williton village to Bridgwater, and a minor road crosses the railway on the level in front of it.

## Doniford Halt                                    7, B2

| Previous name | Doniford Beach Halt | This is a request stop |
|---|---|---|
| Opened | 6 May 1988 | and was built to serve the holiday parks and |
| P&P P&PC | No 30 pp142, 143 WSR pp45, 46; P&PC WSR(2) pp48, 49 | camping sites in the vicinity. |
| Operator          original | WSR | |
| current | WSR | |

Traditional GWR materials were used in the construction of the halt: the platform came from Montacute and the 'pagoda'-style waiting shelter from Cove. The date is 9 June 2009.

## Watchet                                                          7, B2

| Opened | 31 March 1862 | Although the station itself is well presented, the immediate surroundings are not very picturesque. The station is well placed in the centre of the village, but the location is cramped. Most new housing development has taken place on the east side of the village towards Doniford, which is only about a mile away. |
|---|---|---|
| Closed | 4 January 1971 | |
| Reopened | 28 August 1976 | |
| P&P P&PC | No 30 p144 WSR pp47-52; WSR(2) pp52-57 | |
| Operator original | GWR | |
| current | WSR | |

Watchet station on 9 June 2009.

Class 35 'Hymek' diesel-hydraulic locomotive No D7017 takes a freight train towards Williton on the same day.

| Washford | | 7, B2 |
|---|---|---|
| **Previous name** | Washford for Cleeve Abbey | This is another superb station, situated by the side of the main road to Minehead. |
| **Opened** | 16 July 1874 | |
| **Closed** | 4 January 1971 | |
| **Reopened** | 28 August 1976 | |
| **P&PC** | WSR pp54-58; WSR(2) pp59-66 | |
| **Operator** original | GWR | |
| current | WSR | |

The former goods yard, where several interesting wagons can be seen, is home to the Somerset & Dorset Railway Trust, and contains wagons and vans representing pre- and post-Grouping companies, BR and some private owners.

| Blue Anchor | | 7, B2 |
|---|---|---|
| **Previous name** | Bradley Gate | This station is virtually on the seafront of this pleasant village, and there is yet another passing loop here. |
| **Opened** | 16 July 1874 | |
| **Closed** | 4 January 1971 | |
| **Reopened** | 28 August 1976 | |
| **P&P** **P&PC** | No 30 p145 WSR pp59-66; WSR(2) pp67, 68 | |
| **Operator** original | GWR | |
| current | WSR | |

Blue Anchor on 9 June 2009.

The passing loop is frequently used during busy periods and in instances of late running.

| Dunster | | 7, B2 |
|---|---|---|
| Opened | 16 July 1874 | The station is not very conveniently located for the village, but the walk is worthwhile. It is at Dunster that the railway company prints Edmondson-style card tickets for its own use and for other railway companies. The goods yard is still used for the storage of stock and by the engineers' department. |
| Closed | 4 January 1971 | |
| Reopened | 28 August 1976 | |
| P&P P&PC | No 30 p146 WSR pp68-71; WSR(2) pp69-74 | |
| Operator original | GWR | |
| current | WSR | |

The diesel unit is a former BR test train known as IRIS 2, converted from two Class 101 coaches. It was purchased from BR in 2008 and was used by the WSR permanent way department. It has since been transferred to the Barry Island Railway. In the distance, a 'Hymek' locomotive approaches on 9 June 2009.

An 0-4-0 diesel-hydraulic locomotive stands outside the goods shed with a train of ballast wagons. This is one of two such locomotives based here.

| Minehead | | 7, B2 |
|---|---|---|
| **Opened** | 16 July 1874 | Minehead station is in a first-class position for holidaymakers, with both the beach and town in the immediate vicinity. The station is at least as busy as it was in late BR days and it seems extraordinary that the line was ever closed. Minehead is the administrative headquarters of the WSR |
| **Closed** | 4 January 1971 | |
| **Reopened** | 28 August 1976 | |
| **P&P** **P&PC** | No 30 p147 WSR pp72-93; WSR(2) pp75, 76, 84-89 | |
| **Operator original** | GWR | |
| **current** | WSR | |

The end of the journey for No 4160. To the left is Class '4500' No 5553.

Looking towards the buffer stops on 9 June 2009 gives a good indication of the extensive facilities at Minehead. The second vehicle under the tarpaulin is from a diesel unit, and the shunter beyond is Class 04 No D2271.

A closer view of the station shows Class 03 No D2133 with its back to the camera, while the diesel unit on the right consists of three coaches of Classes 115 and 117. The building to the right of the DMU is an extension of the goods shed, built in 1997/98; these two buildings are used as the locomotive depot and works.

The signal box is from Dunster and was moved by rail in 1977. The locomotive in the bay is Class 25 No D7523 *John F. Kennedy*. A working turntable has been installed to the left of the locomotive.

## Templecombe 9, C1

| | | |
|---|---|---|
| **Opened** | 7 May 1860 | Templecombe was one of the stations on the Waterloo-Exeter line that seemed to be deliberately run down in order to justify closure. It was the junction for the SDJR, had a locomotive depot and extensive sidings. Local opposition to closure was strong, but it was 17 years before the station reopened, with funding provided by BR and Somerset County Council. The initial service on reopening was sparse, with no down train for 6 hours on weekdays, while on Sundays the only down train was at 22.14; there were two up trains. There is now an hourly service in each direction, with additional trains at peak periods. Templecombe is thriving, as are all the stations on this line. |
| **Closed** | 7 March 1966 | |
| **Reopened** | 3 October 1983 | |
| **P&P** | No 30 pp112, 113 | |
| **Operator    original** | LSWR | |
| **current** | SWT | |

Class 50 No 50033 *Glorious* pulls away from the station with a Waterloo-Exeter train on 11 August 1990. The station footbridge is in the background and to the right is the former goods shed. Although the line is single through the station, the train is entering the double-track section that runs as far as Yeovil Junction, before becoming single again.

Another Waterloo-Exeter train is seen this time from the old down platform and hauled by No 47801 on 22 April 1992. The footbridge, installed in 1990, is from the ex-LBSCR station of Buxted. where it was made redundant when the line was singled.

Nos 67014 and 67010 top-and-tail a high-speed test train from Eastleigh to Exeter
through Templecombe on 5 October 2004.

The booking office is in the SR-built signal box.

## Feniton                                                                   3, A2

| Previous names | Ottery Road (originally Feniton), Ottery St Mary, Sidmouth Junction | This former junction station consists of a single platform on the original down side; the up platform still exists, but there is no track. In the early years following reopening, there were three trains in the morning and one in the late evening, resulting in a 10-hour gap, and no trains stopped on Sundays. Improvements resulted in most trains stopping on both weekdays and Sundays, giving a bi-hourly service. From December 2009 an hourly service was introduced between Waterloo and Exeter St David's, with every other train calling at Feniton. |
|---|---|---|
| Opened | 19 July 1860 | |
| Closed | 6 March 1967 | |
| Reopened | 3 May 1971 | |
| P&P | No 8 pp35, 36, No 52 pp22, 23 | |
| Operator  original | LSWR | |
| current | SWT | |

Class 50s were used for several years, and on 29 August 1989 No 50028 *Tiger* is on an Exeter to Waterloo train. By this time the former up line had been removed.

These services are currently operated exclusively by Class 159 diesel units, in this instance No 159108 on 18 October 2007.

This is the view at Febiton looking towards Waterloo on the same day, showing the old up platform and the modern box structure on the down platform; this is the booking office, combined with controls for gates, manned by a crossing keeper. On the wall there is a reproduction SR 'target'-style sign displaying the previous name of the station.

## Cranbrook (3, A2)

| Previous name | Broad Clyst |
| --- | --- |
| Opened | 19 July 1860 (original site) |
| Closed | 7 March 1966 |
| Reopening | December 2012 (new site) |
| P&P | No 8 p45, No 52 pp27, 28 |
| Operator    original | LSWR |
| current | SWT |

This station will be at the western edge of the new town of Cranbrook, and is located near Rockbeare, a mile east of the site of the former Broad Clyst station. It will also serve Exeter Airport and a new business park. However, there was no sign whatsoever of building work for either the new town or the station in the autumn of 2010, so the proposed opening date may be unrealistic.

On 1 February 2010 DMU No 159011 passes the site for the new station forming a Waterloo-Exeter train. The site of the original station is well beyond the large tree in the background.

| Pinhoe | | 3, A2 |
|---|---|---|
| Opened | 30 October 1871 | This was the first station on BR to be reopened on an experimental basis under special legislation, and was funded by BR and Devon County Council. No down trains called after 10.30 and on Sundays no trains stopped at all. The experimental status lasted for five years, and Pinhoe is now open on a confirmed basis, and until December 2009 all trains except one stopped on weekdays, but only two on Sundays. Despite increased frequency of trains on the line, only alternate trains now stop at Pinhoe. |
| Closed | 7 March 1966 | |
| Reopened | 16 May 1983 | |
| P&P | No 8 p46, No 52 pp29-31 | |
| Operator original | LSWR | |
| current | SWT | |

Pinhoe station on 18 October 2007.

## Digby & Sowton                                                   3, A2

| Previous name | Clyst St Mary & Digby Halt |
|---|---|
| Opened | 1 June 1908 |
| Closed | 27 September 1948 |
| Reopened | 29 May 1995 on new site |
| P&P | No 52 pp76, 77 |
| Operator original | LSWR |
| current | FGW |

The original halt was immediately north of the present station, whose building was funded by Devon County Council and Tesco Ltd. Its primary purposes are to serve a new housing development, business and retail parks. All trains on the branch stop here, which gives the station a half-hourly service (hourly on Sundays) in each direction. Two more new stations are proposed, one north of here at Hill Barton and the other to the south at Newcourt. Both will serve new housing. This and other stations on the branch are promoted by DCRP.

The approach to the station is by a long ramp, parallel to an identical ramp that is part of a public footpath and cycleway.

On 18 October 2007 single cars of unit No 153377 and an unidentified unit form one of the frequent trains to Exmouth. Most of the branch trains originate from either Barnstaple or Paignton.

| Lympstone Commando | | 3, A2 |
|---|---|---|
| Opened | 3 May 1976 | The station was built exclusively for the Royal Marines Commando Training Centre. It is a request stop and only persons having business at the Centre may alight. There is a military guard adjacent to the platform. |
| Operator original | BR(W) | |
| current | FGW | |

The platform for this station came from Weston Milton Halt, following singling of the line through Weston Milton in 1972 when the down platform became redundant.

A railbus of Class 142 leaves the station on a service from Exmouth to Barnstaple on 18 October 2007. The perimeter fence of the Centre is on the embankment to the left.

1980 TIMETABLES
TORBAY & DARTMOUTH LINE
Paignton-Goodrington Sands-Churston-Dartmouth Ferry & Kingswear
BUCKFASTLEIGH LINE
Buckfastleigh-Staverton-Riverside (Totnes)

**Dart Valley Railway**

STEAM TRAINS

A Great Family Day Out in lovely South Devon

## Paignton Queen's Park      3, B2

| | | |
|---|---|---|
| **Opened** | 1974 | Queen's Park station is the terminus for trains from Kingswear, built on the site of former carriage sidings alongside the ex-GWR station, which is managed by FGW and used by Cross Country and, until December 2009, SWT services. It is planned to rebuild the station in 2012. |
| **P&PC** | PDSR pp49, 50 | |
| **Operator original** | DVR (Torbay Steam Railway) | |
| **current** | DSR | |

The publicity leaflet for the 1980 season, advertising both the Kingswear and Buckfastleigh lines (see page 102).

To the left of the photograph is the former GWR station and to the right the PDSR station. On 17 October 2009 diesel unit No 142063 forms a train to Exmouth, while Class 08 shunter No D3014 *Samson* takes empty stock out of Queen's Park.

The attractive interior of Queen's Park, with Class '4200' No 4277 arriving with a train from Kingswear on the same day. The locomotive was named *Hercules* in 2008.

The approach to Pignton Queen's Park station, which is centrally placed within the town and near the bus station. It is expected to be rebuilt in 2012.

## Britannia Crossing Halt                                      (3, B2)

| Previous names | Steam Ferry Crossing, Kingswear Crossing, Britannia, Britannia Crossing |
|---|---|
| Opened | 1877 |
| Out of use | By 1962 |
| Reopened | 1973 |
| Closed | No records found |
| P&PC | PDSR pages 78, 79 |
| Operator original | GWR |
| on closure | DVR (TSR) |

As far as can be ascertained, the station never appeared in the public timetable. It was used mainly by Royal Navy personnel and workers at the nearby shipyard. It fell out of use in the 1960s, but was used again for a short period in 1973. It was dismantled in 1987.

Britannia Crossing Halt in 1971.
*David Mitchell*

## Totnes Littlehempston

3, B1

| Previous names | Totnes Riverside, Littlehempston Riverside |
|---|---|
| Opened | 1980 |
| Out of use | 1985 |
| Reopened | 1988 |
| Operator original | SDR |
| current | SDR |

Access to the station is only by river or on foot. Trains began running in April 1969, but there were no facilities for alighting or boarding. The platform was built in the 1980s, but still there was no public access. Between 1985 and 1988 SDR trains ran into the BR station, thereafter reverting to using Riverside station. Public access was provided for the first time in 1993 when a footbridge was built over the River Dart. The station has been created in the traditional GWR style, using buildings taken from closed stations elsewhere on the BR network.

GWR Class '5700' No 5786 works an afternoon train to Buckfastleigh on 18 July 2007.
The line to the left is the connection to Network Rail.

The approach to the station on the same day. The water crane is from Leominster.

The main building came from Toller on the Maiden Newton-Bridport branch. It was dismantled in the 1980s and moved to Totnes, which necessitated transporting it by rail from Staverton, as there was (and still is) no road access at Totnes. The station canopy came from Axbridge.

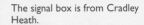

The signal box is from Cradley Heath.

## Napper's Halt                                        (3, B1)

| Opened | | 1997 | The halt is only open on special occasions, when trains stop on request. Because of the low platform, it is only served by auto-trains, and is primarily used by visitors to the local inn and by fishermen. |
|---|---|---|---|
| Operator | original | SDR | |
| | current | SDR | |

Napper's Halt, photographed on 18 July 2007.

## Staverton                                                         3, B1

| Previous name: | Staverton Bridge (originally Staverton) |
|---|---|
| Opened | 1 May 1872 |
| Closed | 3 November 1958 |
| Reopened | 5 April 1969 |
| Operator    original | GWR |
| current | SDR |

Everything about this station is traditional GWR and it is a credit to the railway's employees and volunteers.

Class '1600' pannier tank No 1638, seen here in 1974, was built by BR to a GWR design.

Class '1400' No 1420 waits for the level crossing gates to be opened before proceeding to Totnes in 1974.

Class '4500' No 5526 works a similar train more than 30 years later on 18 July 2007. By this time the station had been fully restored. The bay contains a private-owner open wagon and a GWR goods brake-van.

The same train approaches Staverton on the return journey to Buckfastleigh.

| Buckfastleigh | | | 3, B1 |
|---|---|---|---|
| Opened | | 1 May 1872 | In common with many heritage railway stations, it is much busier now than it was in BR ownership. |
| Closed | | 3 November 1958 | |
| Reopened | | 5 April 1969 | |
| P&P | | No 8 p110 | |
| Operator | original | GWR | |
| | current | SDR | |

Buckfastleigh in the early years of the reinstated service, with No 1420 on a train to Totnes in 1974.

The platform was subsequently lengthened, buildings renovated and sidings installed. The footbridge leads to a picnic area, riverside walk, car park and workshop viewing gallery. Seen on 18 July 2007.

There are signal boxes at both ends of the station. This is the view from the footbridge looking towards Ashburton.

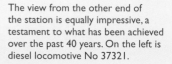

The view from the other end of the station is equally impressive, a testament to what has been achieved over the past 40 years. On the left is diesel locomotive No 37321.

A typical branch-line scene, unchanged for decades.

Buckfastleigh station entrance is enhanced on 18 July 2007 by two classic cars and Routemaster London bus No RM1872. This is one of several buses used to take passengers to the village and Buckfast Abbey.

## Ashburton (3, B1)

| | | |
|---|---|---|
| **Opened** | 1 May 1872 | This station never became part of the SDR, as it was closed prior to change of ownership of the line, which took place on 1 January 1991. The station still exists and is in use as a garage. There are plans by the SDR to reopen the line from Buckfastleigh. |
| **Closed** | 3 November 1958 | |
| **Reopened** | 5 April 1969 | |
| **Closed** | 2 October 1971 | |
| **Operator** original | GWR | |
| last | DVR | |

Ashburton station on 15 April 1956.

## Ivybridge                                                     3, B1

| Previous name | Ivy Bridge | The station is a mile to the east of the original, and is a park-and-ride station, built predominantly for commuters and shoppers to Plymouth. It was funded by the local councils and the European Commission. When first opened the new station had nine trains per day to Plymouth on weekdays and two on Sundays; it currently has nine trains per day to Plymouth and three on Sundays. Passenger numbers have been disappointingly low and the large car park is often almost empty. |
|---|---|---|
| Opened | 15 June 1848 | |
| Closed | 2 March 1959 | |
| Reopened | 15 July 1994 on new site | |
| Operator    original | GWR | |
| current | FGW | |

The 'Royal Duchy' speeds through Ivybridge on its journey to Paddington on 16 July 2007, with motive power provided by Nos 43016 and 43015.

There were plenty of passengers for the single-coach unit No 153369 that formed a Newton Abbot to Plymouth train on the same day.

Occasional freight trains pass through the station, in this instance hauled by No 66203.

## Sampford Courtenay

3, A1

| | |
|---|---|
| **Previous names** | Okehampton Road, Belstone Corner, Sampford Courtenay Halt |
| **Opened** | 8 January 1867 |
| **Closed** | 5 June 1972 |
| **Reopened** | 23 May 2004 |
| **P&P**<br>**P&PC** | No 53 pp92-94;<br>TDL p79 |
| **Operator original** | LSWR |
| **current** | DR |

On first opening the station was the terminus of the LSWR line from Exeter, until it was extended to Okehampton and beyond. Following first closure the line continued to be used by stone trains from Meldon Quarry, and this traffic continues sporadically to the present day. On reopening, the station became the terminus for trains from Okehampton operated by the Dartmoor Railway. It is also served by FGW trains running between Exeter and Okehampton. However, the Dartmoor Railway withdrew all services in 2008, but FGW trains continued to run. Dartmoor Railway services were reinstated by the railway's new owners in 2009, running on summer Saturdays from here to Okehampton and Meldon Quarry. There were plans to run to Yeoford in 2009, but this was postponed until 2010. This did not materialise and at the time of writing there are plans for sister company DCR to run a service to Exeter and London starting in 2011. FGW continues to run a summer Sunday service.

Class '4 TC' No 417 arrives at Sampford Courtenay on 28 August 2004, during the first season of reopening. The unit is propelled by a Class 73 electro-diesel locomotive. There are plenty of cyclists waiting to join the train, known as the 'Dartmoor Pony', to Meldon Quarry. Both Okehampton and Meldon are on a National Cycle Route.

An FGW train from Okehampton, consisting of unit No 150244, leaves the station later the same day.

## Okehampton East

| Opened | Not yet open | Land on which to build this station was purchased by the Dartmoor Railway several years ago, in order to provide a park-and-ride facility. It is the intention of the present company to proceed with the building of the station, although no timescale has been announced. |
| --- | --- | --- |

DEVON RAIL

SPECIAL
SATURDAY EXCURSIONS

Moors-link

Sponsored by
West Devon Borough Council

Okehampton to Exeter

We're getting there

*Left:* The site of the proposed Okehampton East station on 13 August 2010.

*Far left:* A leaflet advertising the summer 1985 services. Trains ran on just four days, with two in each direction.

## Okehampton                                                          3, A1

| Previous name | Okehampton for Hatherleigh | Following closure the station remained derelict for several years, but was transformed under the leadership and vision of the late Roy Gibbs, to become a first-class operational station, with a buffet, model shop, cycle hire and bus/train interchange. It thus gave visitors the opportunity to travel throughout Devon by public transport, and in particular to gain access to Dartmoor. The station (and line) has changed ownership several times since the early days of restoration and was unexpectedly closed at the end of the 2007 season and put up or sale. However, the facilities reopened in 2009. |
| --- | --- | --- |
| Opened | 3 October 1871 | |
| Closed | 5 June 1972; occasional summer services until 23 August 1986 | |
| Reopened | 25 May 1997 for summer weekend services | |
| Closed | End 2007 | |
| Reopened | Spring 2009 | |
| P&P P&PC | No 53 pp6, 96-101 TDL pp83-87 | |
| Operator  original | LSWR | |
| current | DR | |

On 23 August 1986 railbuses Nos 142019 and 142026 are working one of the very occasional trains from Exeter for walkers in the period when the station was in a dilapidated state.

Unit 150239 visited the station several years later on 27 July 1997. By this time the up platform
and main building had been fully restored, but the down platform was still out of use.

This is the station forecourt on 23 July 2000, with three of the connecting buses that form part of the
Sunday Dartmoor Rover experience. Classic buses are regularly used on some of these services.
The station is high above the town and the steep climb continues into the station yard.

There is plenty of variety of motive power; on 28 August 2004 the train to Meldon Quarry is being worked by Nos 47716 and 73134.

Dartmoor Railway and FGW trains meet at Okehampton on 18 September 2005. On the left is unit No 150253 for Exeter, and on the right is former Southern Region Class '3H' No 205032 for Meldon Quarry.

## Meldon Quarry                                          2, A2

| Previous name | Meldon Quarry Halt, Meldon Viaduct | |
|---|---|---|
| Opened | c1890 | The halt was built for railway and quarry workers and their dependants, and an occasional single-coach train ran until the first closure. A new station has now been built nearby, and is at the western extremity of the Dartmoor Railway. Adjacent to the station is a visitor centre, small museum and buffet. |
| Closed | 6 May 1968 | |
| Reopened | 1997 on new site | |
| Closed | April 2008 | |
| Reopened | 10 April 2009 | |
| P&P | No 53 pp106, 107 | |
| Operator original | LSWR | |
| current | DR | |

Viewed from the viaduct end of the station on 18 September 2005 is diesel unit No 205032 in the platform. The quarry is in the background.

Diesel shunter No 08937 occasionally works the 'Dartmoor Pony', as here on 31 August 2003.

Although unnecessary for a single coach, more substantial motive power in the form of electro-diesel No 73134 is also used. In the foreground is the Granite Way, which is part of National Cycle Route No 27 and crosses Meldon Viaduct.

Diesel unit No 205032 has recently been given back its original number of 1132. On 13 August 2010 it waits for cyclists to board prior to running the last service of the day to Okehampton.

## Tavistock                                                        (2, B2)

| | | |
|---|---|---|
| **Previous name** | Tavistock North (originally Tavistock) | The building of a new station for Tavistock on the former LSWR main line to Plymouth is a distinct possibility. It will involve rebuilding the line from Beer Alston and trains could return within five years. Although there is some opposition because a housing development will be permitted as part of a funding arrangement, there is much support from the various councils involved and other official bodies. The original site of the station, which is high above the town beyond a viaduct, has been built on; however, the old station still exists and is currently available for holiday lettings. |
| **Opened** | 1 June 1890 | |
| **Closed** | 6 May 1968 | |
| **Reopened** | On new site, date not yet decided | |
| **P&P** **P&PC** | No 53 p122 TTV pp82-85 | |
| **Operator    original** | LSWR | |
| **future** | FGW | |

This is the site of the proposed station on 16 October 2009, high above the town on the road to Gunnislake.

## Bideford       6, B2

| | |
|---|---|
| **Previous names** | Bideford (New), Bideford for Westward Ho!, Bideford for Hartland |
| **Opened** | 2 November 1855 |
| **Resited** | 10 June 1872 |
| **Closed** | 4 October 1965 |
| **Reopened** | 10 January 1968 |
| **Closed** | 22 January 1968 (see right) |
| **Closed** | 27 January 1983 |
| **P&P** <br> **P&PC** | No 53, p76 <br> Tarka Trail pp38-40 |
| **Operator original** | LSWR |
| **on closure** | BR(W) |

Occasional special trains continued to run after closure to regular services in 1965. In January 1968 the road bridge in Bideford over the River Torridge was closed due to flood damage. A temporary train service was run between Bideford and Torrington to enable people to reach the town. Special passenger trains continued to run very infrequently, the last public train being on 6 November 1982. The last ever train to convey passengers ran on 27 January 1983. For many years there has been pressure to reinstate the line from Barnstaple. The Bideford & Instow Railway Group, established in 1988, developed the station site, which is now under the auspices of the Bideford Railway Heritage Centre Community Interest Company.

The station building (hidden behind coach 76390 from SR electric unit No 3436) is in use as offices. The Tarka Trail, a long-distance footbath and cycleway, passes through the site. The vehicle in the middle distance is SR luggage van No 2142, behind which (out of view) is BR Mark I coach No 4499. The photograph was taken on 18 September 2005.

## Torrington       (6, B2)

| | |
|---|---|
| **Opened** | 18 July 1872 |
| **Closed** | 4 October 1965 |
| **Reopened** | 10 January 1968 |
| **Closed** | 22 January 1968 (see Bideford entry) |
| **Closed** | 27 January 1983 (see Bideford entry) |
| **P&P** <br> **P&PC** | No 8 pp78, 79, No 53 pp76-79 <br> Tarka Trail pp45-47 |
| **Operator original** | LSWR |
| **on closure** | BR(W) |

See the Bideford entry for passenger services. Following closure the station changed hands several times and the main building is used as a restaurant. The Tarka Trail passes through the station.

Track has been relaid through the platform at Torrington and reminders of the railway are prominent throughout the site.

# BODMIN-WADEBRIDGE

## Bodmin General 2, B1

| Previous name | Bodmin |
|---|---|
| Opened | 27 May 1887 |
| Closed | 30 January 1967 |
| Reopened | June 1990 |
| P&P P&PC | No 17 pp30, 31, No 54 pp90, 94 BWR pp16-22 |
| Operator original | GWR |
| current | BWR |

Bodmin General is the terminus of lines from both Bodmin Parkway (formerly Bodmin Road) and Wadebridge. The former is still open and is on the main line to Penzance, but the line towards Wadebridge only reaches Boscarne Junction. Trains run throughout the year, although there are very few in winter. Trains run daily between June and September, with three to Bodmin Parkway and two to Boscarne Junction.

A general view of General on 23 July 2005, looking towards the buffer stops.

This nicely restored station also has an engine shed, works and sidings, all neatly fitting into a rather cramped site. Class '4500' No 5552 is taking water after bringing in a train from Bodmin Parkway, also on 23 July 2005.

The terminus is seen from the yard on 7 July 2006, where LSWR well tank No 30587 is being prepared to work a train to Boscarne Junction.

## Boscarne Junction  1, B2

| | |
|---|---|
| **Previous name** | Boscarne Exchange Platforms |
| **Opened** | 15 June 1964 |
| **Closed** | 18 April 1966 |
| **Reopened** | 2 May 1966 |
| **Closed** | 30 January 1967 |
| **Reopened** | 14 August 1996 |
| **P&P** **P&PC** | No 17 p61, No 54 pp28, 29; BWR pp48, 49 |
| **Operator  original** | BR(W) |
| **current** | BWR |

An interchange station was opened by BR to enable passengers to transfer between trains from Bodmin General and the former LSWR station at Bodmin North. It was part of a rationalisation of services in the area, which were operated by diesel units. The scheme only lasted 2½ years, after which services were withdrawn from both lines. The BWR has built its own terminal station on the site of the platform on the Bodmin General line. The line toward Bodmin North is now part of the Camel Trail, which also extends in the other direction along the trackbed all the way to Padstow. The BWR has aspirations to reopen the line as far as Wadebridge.

This is Boscarne Junction in BR days on 3 July 1961, prior to the building of the station. The line to the left is for Bodmin North and that to the right is for Bodmin General. This was also the location of sidings for the Wenfordbridge china clay traffic, hence the row of wagons on the left.

Two platforms were built immediately beyond the signal box in the vee of the junction, with a normal-height platform on the Bodmin General line and a rail-level platform on the Bodmin North line. A railbus provided a shuttle service from North station to here, passengers then crossing to the higher platform to continue their journey to Wadebridge and Padstow in a conventional diesel unit. There was no road access to the station. In this undated view railcar No W79977 has recently arrived from North station and the staff are standing by the timbers that hardly merited being called a platform. *David Mitchell collection*

A train from Bodmin General
arrives at the present-day
Boscarne Junction on 7 July 2006.

A view of the new station on the same day, looking toward Wadebridge.
A waiting room was opened on the platform in 2009.

## Colesloggett Halt                                                2, B1

| Opened | 17 April 1992 |
| --- | --- |
| P&PC | BWR p13 |
| Operator original | BWR |
| current | BWR |

This is the only intermediate station between Bodmin General and Parkway, and was built to serve a farm park (since closed). It is a useful station for walkers and visitors to Cardingham Woods. Trains to Parkway stop here, but trains do not normally stop in the other direction.

Colesloggett Halt on 7 July 2006.

## Falmouth Town                                    1, C1

| Previous names | | Falmouth, The Dell | This station was opened to replace the terminus of Falmouth, which closed the previous day. It thus became the terminus, but is only a single short platform on an embankment, and proved to be inadequate. The line is promoted by DCRP. |
|---|---|---|---|
| Opened | | 7 December 1970 | |
| Operator | original | BR(W) | |
| | current | FGW | |

Most trains are worked by single-car units of Class 153; on 5 June 2009 it is No 153377.

## Falmouth Docks                                                    1, C2

| | | |
|---|---|---|
| **Previous name** | Falmouth | The station was reopened after five years, to alleviate overcrowding at the new Falmouth Town station. It too is only a single platform, but is much longer, more spacious and has a car park. There have been recent significant improvements on this line and trains run from Truro every 30 minutes on weekdays and approximately hourly on Sundays. |
| **Opened** | 24 August 1863 | |
| **Closed** | 7 December 1970 | |
| **Reopened** | 5 May 1975 | |
| **Operator** original | GWR | |
| current | FGW | |

Falmouth Docks station on 5 June 2009.

# LISKEARD-LOOE ('LOOE VALLEY LINE')

## Moorswater (2, B1)

| | | |
|---|---|---|
| **Previous name** | Liskeard Moorswater | The original station was closed as soon as a new line was built from Coombe to the main line at Liskeard. A new station is proposed on the same site (now known as Moorswater Crossing), as part of a park-and-ride facility for Looe. There is direct access to the site from the A38 trunk road. It is anticipated that a 40-minute-interval service will be provided to Looe. Trains from Liskeard currently run hourly. |
| **Opened** | 11 September 1879 | |
| **Closed** | 15 May 1901 | |
| **Reopened** | Not yet decided | |
| **Operator**     **original** | LCR | |
| **present** | Network Rail | |
| **once opened** | FGW | |

The site of the proposed new Moorswater station on 14 October 2009.